TEARIN

DOWN THE

WALLS

A Practical Guide to Dismantling Toxic Masculinity in Relationships

A book for all genders

**CLAIRE THOMPSON &
CHRISTOPHER FREEMAN**

Breaking the Chains of Toxic Masculinity

We live in a world where masculinity is often defined by aggression, dominance, and emotional suppression. We are taught that "real men" don't cry, don't show vulnerability, and must always be tough and unemotional. These harmful stereotypes are perpetuated by the media, our families, our friends, and our partners, and they can be incredibly damaging to men's mental health, their relationships, and society as a whole.

For too long, we have accepted toxic masculinity as a natural part of being a man. We have watched as it tears apart families and communities, leaving behind a trail of broken relationships and shattered dreams. But it doesn't have to be this way. It's time to break the chains of toxic masculinity and create a new, healthier definition of what it means to be a man.

This book is a practical guide for women in relationships who want to help their partners break free from toxic masculinity and build healthier, more fulfilling relationships. It is also for men who are ready to take the brave step of dismantling toxic masculinity in their own lives and relationships.

Through personal stories, practical exercises, and expert advice, this book will guide you on a journey of growth and transformation. You will learn how to identify toxic behaviors in your relationship, how to overcome shame and insecurity, and how to cultivate empathy, emotional intelligence, and vulnerability. You will also discover communication strategies for building trust, intimacy, and connection with your partner, and learn how to navigate challenges and roadblocks along the way.

But this book is not just about fixing problems. It's about creating a new, positive vision of masculinity that values emotional openness, empathy, and connection. It's about tearing down the walls that separate us from each other and building bridges of understanding and support.

So if you're ready to break free from toxic masculinity and build a stronger, more authentic relationship with your partner, this book is for you. It won't be easy, but it will be worth it. Let's tear down the walls together and create a brighter, more compassionate future for all.

PART 1

Understanding Toxic Masculinity

CHAPTER 1

Defining Toxic Masculinity: What It Is and Why It Matters

Toxic masculinity refers to a set of behaviors, beliefs, and attitudes that are harmful and restrictive to men and those around them. It's a term that has gained increasing recognition and attention in recent years as more people have become aware of its pervasive impact on society.

At its core, toxic masculinity is based on the idea that men must adhere to rigid gender roles and norms in order to be considered "real men." These norms include being aggressive, dominant, and emotionally stoic. Men are often discouraged from expressing emotions other than anger or aggression, and are taught to view vulnerability as a weakness. They are told to prioritize their own desires and needs above those of others, and to maintain control and power in their relationships.

This toxic version of masculinity can manifest in a variety of harmful behaviors and attitudes, including:

- Physical violence or aggression
- Emotional and psychological abuse
- Sexual harassment and assault
- Homophobia and transphobia
- Racism and sexism
- Self-harm and substance abuse
- Emotional detachment and avoidance

1. *Physical violence or aggression:* This form of toxic masculinity is perhaps the most visible and extreme. It can manifest in behaviors such as physical fights, domestic violence, and other acts of aggression. Men who engage in physical violence or aggression often do so to assert their dominance and control over others. This behavior can have devastating consequences for their partners, family members, and others around them.

2. *Emotional and psychological abuse:* This form of toxic masculinity is less visible than physical violence, but can be just as damaging. Emotional and psychological abuse includes behaviors such as gaslighting, manipulation, and verbal attacks. Men who engage in emotional and psychological abuse often do so to maintain control over their partners or to exert power over others. This behavior can lead to long-term emotional and mental health issues for victims.

3. *Sexual harassment and assault:* This form of toxic masculinity is all too common, and can take many forms, including unwanted touching, sexual comments, and sexual assault. Men who engage in sexual harassment or assault often do so to assert their power over others, and may use their position of authority or physical strength to coerce others into sexual acts. Victims of sexual harassment and assault can suffer from long-term emotional and psychological trauma.

4. *Homophobia and transphobia:* This form of toxic masculinity is rooted in the idea that there is a "right" way to be masculine, and that anything outside of that norm is wrong or inferior. Men who engage in homophobia and transphobia often do so to assert their dominance and control over those who don't conform to traditional gender roles. This behavior can create an atmosphere of fear and shame for those who don't fit into traditional gender norms.

5. *Racism and sexism:* These forms of toxic masculinity are rooted in systems of oppression and discrimination, and can take many forms, including discrimination, bias, and prejudice.

Men who engage in racism and sexism often do so to maintain their power and privilege, and to assert their dominance over marginalized groups. This behavior can perpetuate harmful stereotypes and reinforce systems of inequality.

6. Self-harm and substance abuse: This form of toxic masculinity is often overlooked, but can be just as damaging as more visible forms of toxic masculinity. Men who engage in self-harm or substance abuse may do so to numb their emotions or to cope with stress and trauma. This behavior can lead to long-term physical and mental health issues, and can also create a cycle of self-destructive behavior.

7. *Emotional detachment and avoidance:* This form of toxic masculinity is rooted in the idea that men should be emotionally stoic and avoid vulnerability at all costs. Men who engage in emotional detachment and avoidance may struggle to form meaningful connections with others, and may suppress their own emotions in

order to conform to societal expectations. This behavior can create an atmosphere of isolation and disconnection, and can lead to long-term emotional and mental health issues.

These behaviors can have a devastating impact on those around them, especially partners and family members. They can create an atmosphere of fear, isolation, and shame, and can lead to long-term emotional and physical harm.

Toxic masculinity also harms men themselves. By adhering to strict gender norms and suppressing emotions, men may become disconnected from their own needs and desires. They may struggle to form meaningful relationships, to express themselves authentically, and to cope with stress and adversity. In the long term, this can lead to mental health problems, such as depression, anxiety, and addiction.

Why It Matters

Toxic masculinity matters because it is a pervasive problem that affects us all. It perpetuates harmful gender stereotypes and reinforces power imbalances in relationships. It harms men by limiting their emotional expression and authentic self-identity. It harms women and marginalized groups by perpetuating systems of oppression and violence. And it harms society as a whole by creating a culture of fear, aggression, and isolation.

By recognizing and addressing toxic masculinity, we can create a world where everyone is free to express themselves authentically, to form healthy and fulfilling relationships, and to feel safe and valued. We can create a world where masculinity is defined by empathy, compassion, and connection, rather than by aggression and domination.

In the following chapters, we will explore the impact of toxic masculinity on relationships, identify toxic behaviors and attitudes, and provide practical strategies for overcoming them. Together, we can break down the walls of toxic masculinity and create a brighter, more compassionate future for all.

CHAPTER 2

How Toxic Masculinity Impacts Relationships

Toxic masculinity is a complex and multifaceted issue that can have a wide range of negative impacts on all types of relationships, from romantic partnerships to friendships and family connections. In this chapter, we will delve deeper into some of the ways that toxic masculinity can impact relationships, and provide more detailed strategies for overcoming these challenges.

One of the most common ways that toxic masculinity impacts relationships is through communication patterns. Men who adhere to toxic masculinity norms may struggle to express themselves honestly and openly, or may be prone to interrupting or talking over others. This can create a power imbalance in relationships, and can lead to frustration and misunderstanding. In addition, men who adhere to toxic masculinity norms may be more likely to use aggressive or confrontational communication styles, which can escalate conflicts and create further tension in the relationship.

Another way that toxic masculinity can impact relationships is through control and dominance. Men who adhere to toxic masculinity norms may feel a need to control their partners or assert their dominance in the relationship. This can manifest in behaviors such as jealousy, possessiveness, and attempts to limit their partner's freedom and autonomy. These behaviors can be particularly damaging in romantic partnerships, where trust and mutual respect are essential for building a healthy and fulfilling relationship.

Toxic masculinity can also impact intimacy and emotional connection in relationships. Men who adhere to toxic masculinity norms may struggle to express vulnerability or emotion, and may avoid intimacy as a result. This can create a sense of distance and disconnection in the relationship, and can make it difficult for partners to feel truly close to one another. Over time, this lack of emotional connection can erode the foundation of the relationship, and make it more difficult to resolve conflicts or work through challenges together.

In addition, toxic masculinity can impact relationships through expectations around gender roles and responsibilities. Men who adhere to toxic masculinity norms may expect their partners to conform to traditional gender roles, such as taking care of the home and children, while they focus on work or other pursuits. This can create an imbalance in the relationship, and can lead to feelings of resentment and frustration. It can also limit opportunities for both partners to pursue their own interests and passions, and can stifle personal growth and fulfillment.

Overall, toxic masculinity can have a profound and far-reaching impact on relationships, and can make it difficult to form healthy and fulfilling connections with others. In the following chapters, we will explore practical strategies for overcoming the challenges of toxic masculinity in relationships, and for creating a more equitable, respectful, and fulfilling partnership.

Here are some real-life examples of how toxic masculinity can impact relationships:

Example 1: John and Emily

John is a successful businessman who prides himself on his power and dominance. He expects his wife, Emily, to conform to traditional gender roles, such as taking care of the home and children, while he focuses on his career. He is prone to emotional detachment and avoids intimacy, which makes it difficult for Emily to feel truly close to him. Over time, these expectations and behaviors have eroded the foundation of their relationship, and Emily feels trapped and unfulfilled.

Example 2: Sarah and Alex

Alex grew up in a household where aggression and violence were normalized, and he has struggled with anger issues throughout his life. When he and Sarah began dating, he was prone to explosive outbursts and emotional abuse. Despite her best efforts to support him and encourage him to seek help, he continued to escalate his behavior, and eventually became physically violent. Sarah was forced to leave the relationship for her own safety, but the trauma of the experience has had lasting impacts on her mental health and ability to trust others.

Example 3: Miguel and Elena

Miguel grew up with rigid ideas about what it means to be a man, and he has struggled to express vulnerability or emotion throughout his life. When he and Elena began dating, he found it difficult to open up and be truly present with her. Over time, this lack of emotional connection made it difficult for them to resolve conflicts or work through challenges together. Eventually, Elena grew frustrated and felt that Miguel was unable to meet her emotional needs. The relationship ended, leaving both of them feeling unfulfilled and alone.

These are just a few examples of how toxic masculinity can impact relationships in different ways. It is important to recognize that toxic masculinity can manifest in many different behaviors and attitudes, and that it can have a profound and lasting impact on individuals and relationships alike. By understanding the ways in which toxic masculinity can impact our relationships, we can work towards creating healthier, more fulfilling connections with others.

CHAPTER 3

Unpacking Masculine Stereotypes: The Harmful Myths We Believe

Toxic masculinity is deeply intertwined with the stereotypes and expectations that society has created around what it means to be a man. These stereotypes can be harmful not only to men themselves, but also to their partners, families, and communities. In this chapter, we will explore some of the most prevalent masculine stereotypes and myths, and examine the ways in which they contribute to toxic masculinity.

Stereotype 1: Men Should Always Be Strong and Emotionally Detached

One of the most pervasive masculine stereotypes is that men should always be strong, independent, and emotionally detached. This stereotype can make it difficult for men to express vulnerability or emotion, and can lead to feelings of isolation and disconnection. It can also contribute to toxic behaviors such as emotional abuse and neglect, as men struggle to connect with their partners and deal with their own emotions in healthy ways.

Stereotype 2: Real Men Don't Cry or Show Weakness

Another common stereotype is that real men don't cry or show weakness. This stereotype can be incredibly damaging, as it discourages men from seeking help or support when they are struggling. It can also contribute to toxic behaviors such as aggression and violence, as men may feel that expressing vulnerability or emotion is a sign of weakness and may lash out as a result.

Stereotype 3: Men Should Be Dominant and Aggressive

Another harmful stereotype is that men should be dominant and aggressive. This stereotype can lead to behaviors such as physical violence or emotional abuse, as men may feel that they need to assert their dominance in order to be seen as "real men." It can also make it difficult for men to form healthy, equal partnerships with their partners, as they may feel that they need to be in control at all times.

Stereotype 4: Men Should Be Providers and Breadwinners

The stereotype that men should be providers and breadwinners can be particularly harmful, as it can lead to feelings of pressure and inadequacy in men who are unable to meet these expectations. It can also make it difficult for men to form equal partnerships with their partners, as they may feel that they need to be the primary financial providers in order to be seen as "real men."

Stereotype 5: Men Should Be Sexually Aggressive and Promiscuous

The stereotype that men should be sexually aggressive and promiscuous can be particularly harmful to both men and their partners. This stereotype can make it difficult for men to form healthy, respectful sexual relationships, as they may feel pressure to conform to aggressive or exploitative sexual behavior. It can also contribute to behaviors such as sexual harassment or assault, as men may feel entitled to take what they want without regard for their partner's feelings or consent.

Stereotype 6: Men Should Be Invulnerable and Impervious to Pain

The stereotype that men should be invulnerable and impervious to pain can be particularly damaging, as it can make it difficult for men to seek help or support when they are struggling. This stereotype can also contribute to behaviors such as substance abuse or self-harm, as men may feel that they need to numb their emotions or mask their pain in order to be seen as "real men."

Stereotype 7: Men Should Be Hyper-Competitive and Dominant

The stereotype that men should be hyper-competitive and dominant can contribute to behaviors such as aggression, bullying, and belittling others. This stereotype can also make it difficult for men to form healthy, collaborative relationships, as they may feel the need to constantly assert their dominance or "win" at all costs. It is important for men and their partners to recognize that cooperation, respect, and equality are essential components of healthy relationships and communities, and that hyper-competition and dominance are not necessary for success or fulfillment.

By unpacking these masculine stereotypes and examining the ways in which they contribute to toxic masculinity, we can begin to challenge and dismantle them. It is important for men and their partners to recognize that vulnerability, emotion, and equality are essential components of healthy relationships, and that these qualities should be celebrated and valued rather than seen as weaknesses. By working to create a more inclusive and accepting view of masculinity, we can build stronger, more fulfilling relationships and communities for everyone.

PART 2

Identifying Toxic Behaviors in Your Relationship

CHAPTER 4

The Signs of Toxic Masculinity: Identifying Harmful Behaviors in Your Partner

Identifying toxic masculinity in your relationship can be a difficult and sometimes painful process. It requires an honest assessment of your partner's behavior and a willingness to recognize harmful patterns and attitudes. Here are some signs of toxic masculinity to watch out for in your relationship:

1. ***Physical violence or aggression:*** This can include hitting, shoving, or other forms of physical intimidation or violence.

It may also involve the destruction of property or other aggressive behavior.

2. ***Emotional and psychological abuse:*** This can include verbal abuse, such as name-calling, belittling, or humiliating your partner. It may also involve gaslighting or manipulating your partner's emotions in order to control them.

3. ***Sexual harassment and assault:*** This can include unwanted sexual advances, touching, or other forms of sexual behavior without your partner's consent. It may also involve coercion or pressure to engage in sexual behavior.

4. ***Homophobia and transphobia:*** This can include derogatory comments or attitudes toward LGBTQ+ individuals, or a refusal to accept or support your partner's sexual orientation or gender identity.

5. ***Racism and sexism:*** This can include discriminatory comments or attitudes toward individuals based on their race or gender. It may also involve dismissing or belittling the experiences or perspectives of individuals from marginalized groups.

6. ***Self-harm and substance abuse:*** This can include behaviors such as drug or alcohol abuse, cutting, or other forms of self-harm. It may be a sign that your partner is struggling with underlying emotional or mental health issues.

7. ***Emotional detachment and avoidance:*** This can include a lack of emotional intimacy or connection in your relationship. Your partner may seem distant or uninterested in your feelings or experiences, or may avoid talking about emotions altogether.

8. ***Control and possessiveness:*** Your partner may try to control who you spend time with, where you go, and what you wear. They may also become possessive or jealous, even when there is no reason to be.

9. ***Expecting traditional gender roles:*** Your partner may expect you to fulfill traditional gender roles, such as cooking, cleaning, and caring for children, regardless of your own desires or abilities. They may also dismiss or belittle your accomplishments or career aspirations.

10. ***Refusal to apologize or take responsibility:*** Your partner may refuse to acknowledge their mistakes or apologize for their behavior. They may blame you or others for their actions, or minimize the impact of their behavior on your relationship.

11.   ***Hyper masculinity:*** Your partner may place a high value on traditional masculine traits, such as physical strength, dominance, and emotional stoicism. They may view vulnerability or sensitivity as weakness, and may pressure you to conform to gender norms.

12.   ***Disrespect for boundaries:*** Your partner may ignore your boundaries or push you to do things that you are uncomfortable with. They may also try to pressure you into sex or other intimate activities.

13.   ***Gaslighting***: Your partner may deny or minimize your experiences, feelings, or perceptions, and may try to make you doubt your own memory or judgment.

14.   ***Anger issues:*** Your partner may have a short fuse, and may become angry

or aggressive over minor issues. They may also use anger to intimidate or control you.

15.   ***Dismissive or contemptuous behavior:*** Your partner may show little interest in your thoughts, feelings, or opinions, and may dismiss them as unimportant or irrelevant. They may also show contempt or disrespect for you or others.

16.   ***Intimidation or threats:*** Your partner may use intimidation or threats to get their way or to control you. They may also make threats of violence or harm.

17.   ***Lack of empathy:*** Your partner may show little concern for your feelings or well-being, and may be unable or unwilling to see things from your perspective.

41

18.   ***Substance abuse***: Your partner may use drugs or alcohol as a way to cope with their emotions or to escape from problems, and may become abusive or violent when under the influence.

19.   ***Control and manipulation:*** Your partner may try to control various aspects of your life, including your social life, finances, and daily routine. They may also use manipulation tactics, such as guilt-tripping or emotional blackmail, to get their way.

20.   ***Objectification and entitlement:*** Your partner may view you or other people as objects to be used for their own pleasure or benefit, and may feel entitled to sex, attention, or other forms of gratification. They may also lack respect for boundaries and consent, and may pressure or coerce you into sexual acts or other behaviors.

If you notice any of these signs in your partner, it is important to seek help and support. This may involve speaking with a therapist, joining a support group, or reaching out to a domestic violence or abuse hotline. It is also important to set boundaries and communicate clearly with your partner about what behaviors are unacceptable in your relationship. Remember that you deserve to be treated with respect and kindness, and that you have the right to prioritize your own well-being and safety.

CHAPTER 5

The Impact of Toxic Masculinity on Intimacy and Communication

Toxic masculinity can have a significant impact on the intimacy and communication in your relationship. Here are some ways it can manifest:

1. ***Emotional detachment***: Toxic masculinity often teaches men to suppress their emotions and avoid vulnerability. This can lead to emotional detachment in relationships, making it difficult to connect with your partner on a deep and meaningful level.

2. *Lack of communication:* Toxic masculinity can also encourage men to avoid talking about their feelings or seeking help when they need it. This can lead to a lack of communication in the relationship, making it difficult to address issues or work through challenges together.

3. *Power imbalances:* Toxic masculinity often places a premium on dominance and control, which can create power imbalances in relationships. This can lead to a lack of equality and mutual respect, which can erode intimacy over time.

4. *Disrespect for boundaries:* Toxic masculinity may also make it difficult for men to respect their partner's boundaries, whether they be physical or emotional. This can create an unsafe and uncomfortable environment for your

partner, which can lead to a breakdown in intimacy.

5. ***Pressure to conform:*** Toxic masculinity can create pressure for men to conform to traditional gender roles, which can be limiting and harmful. This can make it difficult to express yourself authentically in the relationship and can create a sense of resentment or dissatisfaction over time.

6. ***Lack of empathy:*** Toxic masculinity can also contribute to a lack of empathy towards others, including your partner. This may manifest as dismissiveness towards their feelings or experiences, or an inability to truly understand or relate to them.

7. ***Inability to apologize or take responsibility:*** Toxic masculinity can make it difficult for men to apologize or

take responsibility for their actions. This may be due to a fear of appearing weak or vulnerable, or a belief that admitting fault is a sign of weakness.

8. **Aggressive communication:** Toxic masculinity may also contribute to aggressive communication styles, such as yelling, name-calling, or other forms of verbal abuse. This can create a hostile and unsafe environment in the relationship, and can make it difficult for both partners to communicate effectively.

9. **Objectification of women:** Toxic masculinity often reinforces the idea that women are objects to be desired or conquered. This can lead to disrespectful or harmful behavior towards women, and can create a lack of trust and intimacy in the relationship.

10. ***Disregard for consent:*** Toxic masculinity may also contribute to a lack of respect for consent and boundaries, particularly in sexual situations. This can create a dangerous and harmful environment for your partner, and can erode the trust and intimacy in the relationship.

By being aware of these harmful behaviors and their impact on your relationship, you can take steps to address them and work towards building a healthier and more fulfilling partnership. This may involve seeking support from a therapist or counselor, educating yourself on healthy communication and relationship skills, and making a commitment to treating your partner with respect, empathy, and understanding. Remember that change is possible, and that by taking responsibility for your actions and behaviors, you can create a more positive and loving relationship with your partner.

For further case study, here are some real-life examples of how toxic masculinity can impact intimacy and communication in relationships:

A. **Dismissive behavior:** John and Sarah have been in a relationship for several months. Whenever Sarah tries to talk to John about her feelings or concerns, he dismisses her and tells her that she's overreacting. This behavior makes Sarah feel unheard and undervalued, and it creates a barrier to intimacy and communication in their relationship.

B. **Aggressive communication:** Mark and Lisa have been married for several years. Whenever they argue, Mark yells, curses, and throws things. This behavior is intimidating and frightening for Lisa, and it creates a hostile environment in their home. This aggressive communication style erodes the trust and intimacy in their relationship.

C. ***Objectification of women:*** David and Rachel have been dating for a few months. Whenever they go out, David constantly comments on other women's appearances and talks about how he would like to be with them. This behavior makes Rachel feel objectified and disrespected, and it creates a lack of trust and intimacy in their relationship.

D. ***Disregard for consent:*** Mike and Kelly have been in a relationship for a while. One night, Mike initiates sexual activity without asking for Kelly's consent. This behavior is a violation of Kelly's boundaries and creates a dangerous and harmful environment for her. It erodes the trust and intimacy in their relationship.

E. ***Emotional detachment:*** Tom and Emily have been married for several years. Whenever Emily tries to talk to Tom about their relationship or her feelings, he shuts down and becomes emotionally distant. This behavior creates a lack of intimacy and communication in their relationship and can lead to feelings of loneliness and isolation for Emily.

CHAPTER 6

Deconstructing Traditional Gender Roles: The Harmful Effects on Relationships

Traditional gender roles have long been a part of society, dictating how men and women are expected to behave in relationships. However, these gender roles can be harmful and limiting, particularly when they reinforce toxic masculinity. Here are some of the harmful effects traditional gender roles can have on relationships:

1. *Limits individual expression:* Traditional gender roles can create a narrow definition of what it means to be a man or woman, limiting individual

expression and creating pressure to conform. This can lead to feelings of dissatisfaction or resentment in the relationship, particularly if one partner feels constrained by traditional gender roles.

2. **Reinforces power imbalances:** Traditional gender roles often place men in positions of power and control, while women are expected to be submissive and obedient. This can create power imbalances in relationships, making it difficult for partners to communicate and connect on an equal footing.

3. **Restricts emotional expression:** Traditional gender roles often dictate that men should be strong and stoic, while women are expected to be nurturing and emotional. This can make it difficult for men to express their emotions and connect with their partner on a deeper

level, leading to emotional detachment and a lack of intimacy in the relationship.

4. ***Creates unrealistic expectations:*** Traditional gender roles can create unrealistic expectations about what men and women should be like in a relationship, leading to disappointment and frustration when these expectations are not met. This can put undue pressure on both partners and make it difficult to build a healthy and fulfilling relationship.

5. ***Limits career opportunities:*** Traditional gender roles often dictate that men should be breadwinners and women should be homemakers. This can limit career opportunities for women and create financial dependence, which can be a source of stress and conflict in the relationship.

6. ***Limits shared responsibilities:*** Traditional gender roles can also create limitations on shared responsibilities in a relationship. For instance, men may feel that they are not responsible for household chores, child-rearing, or emotional labor, while women are expected to take on these tasks. This can create resentment and tension in the relationship, as well as an unequal distribution of labor that can be damaging to the partnership.

7. ***Perpetuates stereotypes:*** Traditional gender roles often perpetuate harmful stereotypes about men and women, reinforcing the idea that men are dominant and women are submissive. These stereotypes can have long-lasting effects on the way that men and women view themselves and their roles in the relationship, leading to an imbalance of power and a lack of emotional connection.

8. ***Limits communication:*** Traditional gender roles can make it difficult for partners to communicate effectively, particularly if one partner feels that they must conform to gender stereotypes in order to be accepted. This can make it difficult to share feelings, needs, and desires in the relationship, leading to misunderstandings and conflicts that can damage the partnership.

Deconstructing traditional gender roles can be challenging, as they are deeply ingrained in society and culture. However, it is an important step in building a healthy and fulfilling relationship, as it allows both partners to express themselves freely and build a partnership based on equality and mutual respect. This may involve exploring your own gender identity and values, challenging gender stereotypes and expectations, and working to create a more balanced and equitable distribution of labor in the relationship. With time and effort, it is possible to overcome the harmful effects of traditional gender roles and build a relationship that is healthy, loving, and fulfilling for both partners.

PART 3

Overcoming Toxic Masculinity in Your Relationship

CHAPTER 7

Building Trust and Safety: The Foundation for Overcoming Toxic Masculinity

In order to overcome toxic masculinity in your relationship, it is crucial to establish a foundation of trust and safety. This means creating an environment where both partners feel heard, respected, and valued, and where they can communicate openly and honestly without fear of judgment or harm. Building trust and safety can be challenging, particularly if there has been a history of toxic behaviors in the relationship. However, with time and effort, it is possible to create a safe and supportive environment that allows both partners to grow and thrive.

One key aspect of building trust and safety is creating clear and healthy boundaries. This means establishing guidelines for behavior and communication that are respectful, supportive, and compassionate. It also means being willing to hold each other accountable when those boundaries are crossed, and working together to find solutions that support the growth and well-being of both partners.

Another important aspect of building trust and safety is developing effective communication skills. This means learning to listen actively, express yourself clearly and honestly, and communicate in a way that is respectful and non-judgmental. It also means being willing to take responsibility for your own emotions and behaviors, and working to communicate your needs and desires in a way that is clear and constructive.

Ultimately, building trust and safety requires a willingness to be vulnerable and authentic with each other. It means being willing to share your feelings, fears, and desires, and to listen to your partner with an open heart and mind. It also means being willing to work through conflicts and challenges in a way that is supportive and constructive, and to prioritize the health and well-being of the relationship above all else.

Building trust and safety in a relationship requires effort from both partners. It involves creating an environment where both individuals feel comfortable and respected, and where they can communicate their needs and concerns without fear of judgment or retaliation. This can be particularly challenging in relationships where there has been a history of toxic behaviors, such as emotional or physical abuse, because trust has been broken and safety has been compromised.

To begin building trust and safety, it is important to establish clear and healthy boundaries. This means setting guidelines for behavior and communication that are respectful, supportive, and compassionate. It also means being willing to hold each other accountable when those boundaries are crossed, and working together to find solutions that support the growth and well-being of both partners. This may involve seeking the help of a therapist or counselor who can provide guidance and support in building healthy boundaries and communication skills.

Another important aspect of building trust and safety is developing effective communication skills. This means learning to listen actively, express yourself clearly and honestly, and communicate in a way that is respectful and non-judgmental. It also means being willing to take responsibility for your own emotions and behaviors, and working to communicate your needs and desires in a way that is clear and constructive. Effective communication is the cornerstone of any healthy relationship, and it is essential for building trust and safety.

In addition to setting boundaries and developing effective communication skills, building trust and safety also involves practicing empathy and compassion. This means being willing to put yourself in your partner's shoes, and to understand and validate their feelings and experiences. It also means being willing to offer support and encouragement, and to create an environment where both partners feel valued and appreciated.

Finally, building trust and safety requires a willingness to be vulnerable and authentic with each other. This means being willing to share your feelings, fears, and desires, and to listen to your partner with an open heart and mind. It also means being willing to work through conflicts and challenges in a way that is supportive and constructive, and to prioritize the health and well-being of the relationship above all else.

In summary, building trust and safety is essential for overcoming toxic masculinity in a relationship. It involves setting clear and healthy boundaries, developing effective communication skills, practicing empathy and compassion, and being willing to be vulnerable and authentic with each other. While it may take time and effort, the rewards of a healthy and loving relationship are well worth the investment.

CHAPTER 8

Practicing Empathy and Emotional Intelligence

One of the most critical steps in overcoming toxic masculinity in relationships is developing emotional intelligence and empathy. Unfortunately, traditional gender roles often discourage men from expressing their emotions or understanding those of their partners. As a result, men may struggle to connect with their emotions and the emotions of others, leading to a lack of empathy and poor communication skills.

Emotional intelligence is the ability to identify, understand, and manage one's emotions effectively. It also involves being able to recognize and respond appropriately to the emotions of others. When partners have high levels of emotional intelligence, they can communicate more effectively, resolve conflicts more easily, and build deeper, more meaningful connections.

Empathy, on the other hand, is the ability to put oneself in another person's shoes and understand their feelings and experiences. Empathy is essential in relationships because it helps partners understand each other better, leading to increased intimacy and trust.

To develop emotional intelligence and empathy, both partners need to practice active listening, self-awareness, and validation. Active listening involves paying attention to what the other person is saying and trying to understand their point of view. Self-awareness involves being honest about one's emotions and reactions and understanding how they affect the relationship. Validation means acknowledging and accepting each other's feelings and experiences, even if they differ from one's own.

In addition to active listening, self-awareness, and validation, there are other ways to practice empathy and emotional intelligence in relationships. Some of these strategies include:

1. **Reflective questioning:** Instead of assuming one knows what their partner is feeling or thinking, ask open-ended questions to clarify and understand their perspective better. Reflective questioning involves asking questions that prompt the other person to elaborate on their thoughts and feelings, such as "Can you tell me more about that?" or "How did that make you feel?"

2. **Non-judgmental attitude:** To cultivate empathy, one must approach the other person with a non-judgmental attitude. It means accepting and acknowledging the

other person's thoughts and feelings without criticizing, dismissing, or invalidating them. Being non-judgmental means listening and responding with kindness, understanding, and compassion.

3. *Embracing vulnerability:* Toxic masculinity often discourages men from being vulnerable or showing emotions. However, being vulnerable can help build intimacy and trust in a relationship. By sharing their emotions and experiences, both partners can develop a deeper understanding of each other and create a safe space for emotional expression.

4. *Practicing mindfulness:* Mindfulness involves being present in the moment and paying attention to one's thoughts and feelings without judgment. Practicing mindfulness can help one regulate their emotions and respond to their partner in

a more empathetic and compassionate manner. Mindfulness practices such as meditation or deep breathing exercises can help reduce stress and improve emotional regulation.

By practicing empathy and emotional intelligence, couples can overcome toxic masculinity in their relationships. They can learn to communicate more effectively, understand each other's emotions, and build deeper connections. Over time, these practices can lead to a healthier, more fulfilling relationship that is free from harmful stereotypes and behaviors.

CHAPTER 9

Communication Strategies for Healthy, Connected Relationships

Effective communication is essential for building healthy, connected relationships. Unfortunately, toxic masculinity can often make it difficult for men to express their emotions and communicate in a healthy way. In this chapter, we will explore communication strategies that can help you overcome toxic masculinity in your relationship and foster deeper connection and understanding.

1. ***Practice active listening:*** When your partner is speaking, focus on what they are saying and try to understand their

point of view. Put your own thoughts and opinions aside and listen without judgment or interruption.

2. ***Validate your partner's feelings***: Even if you don't agree with your partner's emotions or experiences, it's essential to acknowledge and accept them. This can help your partner feel heard and validated, which can strengthen your relationship.

3. ***Practice self-awareness:*** Be honest with yourself about your own emotions and reactions. Understand how they may be affecting your relationship and work to manage them in healthy ways.

4. ***Practice empathy:*** Put yourself in your partner's shoes and try to understand their feelings and experiences. Ask questions to gain a deeper understanding of their perspective.

5. **Use "I" statements**: Instead of blaming or accusing your partner, use "I" statements to express how you feel. For example, say "I feel hurt when you do X" instead of "You always do X, and it's so frustrating."

6. ***Be open to feedback:*** Listen to your partner's feedback and be willing to make changes to improve your relationship.

7. ***Take responsibility for your actions:*** If you make a mistake or hurt your partner, take responsibility and apologize. Work together to find ways to avoid similar situations in the future.

8. ***Practice mindfulness:*** Pay attention to your thoughts and emotions in the present moment, and be aware of how they might be affecting your interactions with your partner. Taking a few deep

breaths or engaging in relaxation techniques like meditation or yoga can also help you stay calm and centered.

9. **Seek to understand your partner's perspective:** When you are having a disagreement or conflict, take the time to understand your partner's point of view. Try to see things from their perspective, and ask questions to gain a deeper understanding of how they are feeling.

10. **Practice forgiveness**: It's important to forgive your partner when they make mistakes or hurt you. Holding onto grudges or resentments can damage your relationship over time. By practicing forgiveness, you can let go of negative emotions and move forward together.

11. **Take care of yourself:** Practicing empathy and emotional intelligence can be emotionally taxing. Make sure to take

care of yourself by practicing self-care and setting healthy boundaries.

12. **_Practice gratitude:_** Show appreciation for your partner and the positive aspects of your relationship. This can help build feelings of love, connection, and positivity.

13. **_Practice assertiveness:_** Assertiveness means standing up for yourself and expressing your needs and boundaries in a clear and respectful way. This can be difficult for men who have been taught to prioritize others' needs over their own, but it is essential for building healthy relationships.

14. **_Avoid stonewalling or defensiveness:_** Stonewalling is withdrawing or shutting down during a conflict, while defensiveness involves responding with anger or deflection when

feeling criticized. Both behaviors can be harmful to relationships, so it's important to practice staying open and engaged during difficult conversations.

15.   *Use humor and positivity:* Humor and positivity can help defuse tension and create a more relaxed, connected atmosphere during communication. However, it's important to make sure that the humor is not used to dismiss or invalidate your partner's feelings.

16.   *Seek professional help if needed:* If you are struggling to communicate effectively or have difficulty managing your emotions, seeking the help of a mental health professional can be beneficial. They can provide guidance and support for developing healthy communication skills.

By practicing these communication strategies, you can overcome toxic masculinity in your relationship and build a healthier, more connected bond with your partner.

CHAPTER 10

Cultivating Vulnerability and Authenticity in Your Relationship

Toxic masculinity often leads men to believe that they must always be strong, tough, and invulnerable. This can make it difficult for men to open up emotionally and be vulnerable with their partners, which can lead to a breakdown in intimacy and trust in the relationship.

In this chapter, we will explore the importance of cultivating vulnerability and authenticity in your relationship, and how it can help you overcome toxic masculinity.

Understanding Vulnerability

Vulnerability can be defined as the state of being exposed to the possibility of harm or injury. In a relationship, vulnerability means being open and honest with your partner about your thoughts, feelings, and fears, even if it makes you feel uncomfortable or scared.

Cultivating vulnerability requires trust and safety in the relationship. It is important for both partners to feel that they can be vulnerable with each other without fear of judgement or criticism.

Embracing Authenticity

Authenticity means being true to oneself and one's feelings. In a relationship, authenticity means being honest with your partner about who you are, what you want, and what you need from the relationship.

Toxic masculinity can make it difficult for men to express their true selves, as they may feel pressure to conform to traditional gender roles and expectations. However, embracing authenticity is essential for building a healthy and fulfilling relationship.

How to Cultivate Vulnerability and Authenticity in Your Relationship

1. *Practice active listening:* One of the most important ways to cultivate vulnerability and authenticity in your relationship is by actively listening to your partner. This means giving them your full attention, without judgement or interruption, and seeking to understand their perspective.

2. *Be honest about your feelings:* If you want your partner to be vulnerable and

authentic with you, you need to do the same. Be honest about your feelings, even if they are uncomfortable or difficult to express.

3. **Practice self-reflection:** Take the time to reflect on your own thoughts, feelings, and behaviors. This can help you understand yourself better, and make it easier to express your true self to your partner.

4. **Challenge traditional gender roles:** Toxic masculinity often reinforces traditional gender roles and expectations. Challenge these roles by exploring new ways of expressing your masculinity, and by encouraging your partner to do the same.

5. **Seek support:** Overcoming toxic masculinity is not easy, and it may be helpful to seek support from a therapist

or counselor. They can help you navigate the challenges of cultivating vulnerability and authenticity in your relationship.

Cultivating vulnerability and authenticity in your relationship is essential for overcoming toxic masculinity. It requires trust, safety, and a willingness to be honest and open with your partner. By practicing active listening, being honest about your feelings, practicing self-reflection, challenging traditional gender roles, and seeking support, you can create a relationship that is healthy, fulfilling, and free from toxic masculinity.

CHAPTER 11

Overcoming Shame and Insecurity: Strategies for Building Self-Worth and Confidence

Toxic masculinity can be rooted in feelings of shame and insecurity. Men may feel pressure to meet societal expectations of what it means to be a man, and when they fall short of those expectations, they may feel inadequate and ashamed. These feelings can lead to harmful behaviors and a toxic cycle of trying to prove oneself as "man enough." In this chapter, we will explore strategies for overcoming shame and insecurity and building self-worth and confidence.

A. The importance of recognizing and challenging societal messages that contribute to shame and insecurity.

The impact of shame and insecurity can be devastating for individuals and relationships alike. In many cases, these emotions stem from societal messages that can be difficult to escape. Unrealistic beauty standards, toxic masculinity norms, and the belief that vulnerability is weakness are just a few examples of messages that can contribute to feelings of inadequacy and self-doubt.

It's important to recognize and challenge these messages in order to overcome shame and insecurity. This can involve questioning the underlying assumptions that support these beliefs, and seeking out alternative perspectives and role models that offer a more positive and affirming view of oneself and one's abilities.

For example, rather than buying into the idea that a certain body type or physical appearance is necessary for attractiveness and acceptance, one can focus on developing and valuing other qualities, such as kindness, intelligence, and humor. Similarly, rather than accepting toxic masculinity norms that promote aggression and emotional detachment, one can explore healthier forms of masculinity that emphasize compassion, vulnerability, and emotional expression.

By challenging these messages and exploring new perspectives, individuals can begin to build a more positive sense of self-worth and confidence. This can involve practicing assertiveness, setting boundaries, and celebrating successes in order to cultivate a greater sense of agency and control over one's life and relationships.

However, it's important to recognize that overcoming shame and insecurity can be a challenging and ongoing process, and setbacks and relapses are common. It's important to maintain a growth mindset and to be patient and compassionate with oneself throughout the journey.

In some cases, past traumas or experiences may contribute to shame and insecurity, and seeking professional help may be necessary in order to work through these issues. By addressing these underlying issues and developing a greater sense of self-awareness and self-compassion, individuals can begin to heal and move forward in a more positive and fulfilling direction.

In conclusion, recognizing and challenging societal messages that contribute to shame and insecurity is a crucial step in overcoming toxic masculinity and building healthier relationships. By cultivating self-worth and confidence, individuals can learn to communicate and connect with others in more authentic and meaningful ways, and experience greater satisfaction and fulfillment in their relationships and lives.

B. Strategies for building self-worth.

Part of overcoming shame and insecurity involves building a stronger sense of self-worth. This means recognizing and valuing one's own inherent worth, regardless of external factors or societal messages. Here are some strategies for building self-worth:

1. **Practice self-compassion:** It's easy to be hard on ourselves when we make mistakes or experience setbacks. However, cultivating self-compassion involves treating ourselves with the same kindness, care, and understanding that

we would offer to a close friend. This means acknowledging our mistakes without self-judgment and reminding ourselves that it's okay to make mistakes.

2. *Set and achieve small goals:* Setting small, achievable goals can help build confidence and self-esteem. Celebrate each accomplishment, no matter how small, and use it as motivation to continue working towards bigger goals.

3. *Focus on strengths:* Instead of dwelling on weaknesses or perceived shortcomings, make an effort to recognize and appreciate your strengths. Make a list of your positive qualities and accomplishments, and remind yourself of them regularly.

4. **Practice self-care**: Taking care of oneself physically, emotionally, and mentally is an important part of building

self-worth. This could include things like getting enough sleep, eating a balanced diet, engaging in physical activity, spending time with loved ones, or seeking out therapy or counseling if needed.

By implementing these strategies, individuals can gradually build a stronger sense of self-worth and confidence, which can help them overcome feelings of shame and insecurity in their relationships.

C. The role of therapy and other forms of support.

The impact of shame and insecurity on relationships can be significant, leading to self-doubt, fear of rejection, and a lack of trust in one's partner. Therefore, it is essential to understand how these issues can contribute to harmful behaviors in relationships and the strategies for overcoming them.

One crucial step in overcoming shame and insecurity is recognizing and challenging the societal messages that contribute to these feelings. Unrealistic beauty standards, toxic masculinity norms, and the idea that vulnerability is weakness are just a few examples of messages that can contribute to shame and insecurity. By identifying and challenging these messages, individuals can begin to cultivate a more positive self-image and build self-worth.

Another key strategy for building self-worth and confidence is practicing self-compassion. This involves treating oneself with kindness and understanding rather than self-judgment and criticism. Setting and achieving small goals can also help individuals build self-confidence and a sense of accomplishment. Additionally, focusing on one's strengths rather than weaknesses can help to reframe negative self-talk and build a more positive self-image.

Therapy and other forms of support can also be essential in overcoming shame and insecurity. Cognitive-behavioral therapy, group therapy, and self-help resources can provide individuals with the tools and support needed to challenge negative thought patterns, build self-confidence, and improve their relationships.

However, overcoming shame and insecurity is not always an easy or linear process. Setbacks and relapses can occur, and it is essential to maintain a growth mindset and persevere through difficult times. It is also crucial to acknowledge and address any past traumas or experiences that may be contributing to shame and insecurity and to seek professional help if needed.

Overall, overcoming shame and insecurity is a journey that requires patience, self-compassion, and a willingness to challenge negative thought patterns and societal messages. By building self-worth and confidence, individuals can improve their relationships and experience greater emotional well-being.

D. Ways in which shame and insecurity can contribute to harmful behaviors in relationships.

Shame is the belief that one is fundamentally flawed and not worthy of love or acceptance. In relationships, shame can manifest as feelings of inadequacy or fear of rejection, leading to behaviors such as jealousy, possessiveness, and controlling behavior. Insecurity is a feeling of uncertainty or lack of confidence in oneself or one's abilities, which can lead to behaviors such as defensiveness, avoidance, and self-sabotage.

Overcoming shame and insecurity is crucial for building healthy relationships. It requires a willingness to face and challenge negative beliefs about oneself and to cultivate self-compassion and self-worth. This can be achieved through therapy, self-reflection, and building a support system of trusted friends and family.

By addressing shame and insecurity, individuals can improve their communication and ability to be vulnerable with their partner. This, in turn, leads to increased trust and intimacy in the relationship. Overcoming shame and insecurity also allows individuals to take responsibility for their actions and behaviors, leading to healthier and more fulfilling relationships.

E. Tips for cultivating confidence in oneself and one's relationship.

Building self-worth and confidence is crucial for overcoming toxic masculinity in relationships. Shame and insecurity can often contribute to harmful behaviors, such as control, jealousy, and emotional manipulation. These behaviors can erode trust and create a toxic environment in a relationship.

To overcome these issues, it's important to recognize the root causes of shame and insecurity, which can be deeply ingrained in societal expectations and personal experiences. Therapy or counseling can be helpful in addressing these underlying issues and developing strategies for building self-esteem.

Assertiveness is a key tool for cultivating confidence in oneself and one's relationship. This involves expressing one's needs and desires clearly and respectfully, without resorting to aggression or manipulation. Setting and maintaining healthy boundaries is also important for building confidence and preventing toxic behaviors from creeping into a relationship.

Celebrating successes, both big and small, can also help to build confidence and strengthen a relationship. This could include acknowledging and appreciating each other's accomplishments, expressing gratitude for the positive aspects of the relationship, and finding joy in shared experiences.

F. Challenges and setbacks.

Overcoming shame and insecurity is not an easy task, and it's important to recognize that setbacks and relapses are a normal part of the process. It's common to fall back into old patterns of behavior, especially in moments of stress or conflict.

One of the keys to maintaining progress is to develop a growth mindset. This means recognizing that change is a process and that setbacks are an opportunity to learn and grow. It's important to approach setbacks with curiosity and compassion, rather than judgment or self-criticism.

Another helpful strategy is to practice self-care and self-compassion. This can include things like getting enough rest, engaging in activities that bring joy and fulfillment, and talking to a therapist or support group. Taking care of oneself is essential to building the resilience and emotional strength needed to overcome shame and insecurity.

Finally, it's important to recognize that the journey of overcoming shame and insecurity is ongoing. It's not a destination that can be reached, but a process that requires ongoing effort and attention. By continuing to cultivate confidence, set boundaries, and practice assertiveness, it's possible to build a stronger and healthier relationship with oneself and one's partner.

G. Acknowledging and addressing past traumas.

Acknowledging and addressing past traumas and experiences that contribute to shame and insecurity is an important step towards overcoming toxic masculinity in a relationship. Trauma, such as childhood abuse or neglect, can cause a person to develop negative beliefs about themselves and their worthiness, which can manifest in harmful behaviors towards their partner.

It is important to recognize that healing from past traumas takes time and effort, and it may not be possible to do it alone. Seeking professional help from a therapist or counselor can provide a safe and supportive environment to work through these issues.

In addition to seeking professional help, there are also other ways to address past traumas and experiences. These may include journaling, practicing mindfulness, engaging in physical exercise, and connecting with supportive friends and family members.

It is important to remember that overcoming shame and insecurity is a process, and setbacks and relapses are a normal part of the journey. It is important to maintain a growth mindset and continue to work towards cultivating confidence and self-worth in oneself and in the relationship.

In conclusion, acknowledging and addressing past traumas and experiences is an essential part of overcoming toxic masculinity in a relationship. Seeking professional help and implementing healthy coping strategies can help in the healing process and lead to a more fulfilling and satisfying relationship. By recognizing and addressing feelings of shame and insecurity, men can begin to break the cycle of toxic masculinity and build healthier, more fulfilling relationships.

CHAPTER 12

Strengthening the Bonds: Sexual Intimacy and Connection in Healthy Relationships

Sexual intimacy is an essential aspect of any romantic relationship, and it can play a significant role in building a strong connection between partners. Unfortunately, toxic masculinity often manifests in the realm of sex and can have a profound impact on a couple's sexual relationship. In this chapter, we will explore how toxic masculinity can affect sexual intimacy and provide strategies for cultivating a healthy and fulfilling sex life.

The Impact of Toxic Masculinity on Sexual Intimacy.

Toxic masculinity can have a detrimental impact on a couple's sexual relationship. Men who buy into the idea that they must be aggressive, dominant, and unemotional in their sexual encounters often struggle to create a safe and intimate space with their partner. This can lead to a host of problems, including:

1. ***Lack of communication:*** Men who have been conditioned to believe that they must be dominant in the bedroom may struggle to communicate their desires and boundaries effectively. This can lead to misunderstandings, discomfort, and even sexual assault.

2. ***Performance anxiety:*** Men who feel pressure to perform sexually may experience anxiety or even erectile

dysfunction. This can further exacerbate feelings of shame and inadequacy.

3. **Objectification:** Men who view sex as a conquest may objectify their partners and prioritize their own pleasure over their partner's needs and desires.

Strategies for Cultivating a Healthy and Fulfilling Sex Life

Overcoming toxic masculinity requires a commitment to open communication, vulnerability, and mutual respect. Here are some strategies that can help couples cultivate a healthy and fulfilling sex life:

1. **Communicate openly and honestly:** Communication is essential in any sexual encounter. Men must learn to communicate their desires, boundaries, and concerns openly and honestly. They

must also be willing to listen actively to their partner's needs and desires.

2. **Prioritize consent**: Consent is a critical component of any sexual encounter. Men must learn to respect their partner's boundaries and prioritize their comfort and safety.

3. **Embrace vulnerability:** Vulnerability is key to creating a safe and intimate space in the bedroom. Men must learn to let go of the idea that they must be dominant and in control at all times and embrace vulnerability, trust, and emotional intimacy.

4. **Explore sensuality:** Sex is not just about physical pleasure; it is also about emotional connection and sensuality. Couples can explore sensuality by engaging in activities such as sensual

massage, cuddling, or practicing mindfulness together.

5. ***Prioritize pleasure for both partners:*** Healthy sexual relationships prioritize pleasure for both partners. Men must learn to prioritize their partner's needs and desires and understand that pleasure is a mutual experience.

In conclusion, overcoming toxic masculinity in the realm of sex requires a commitment to communication, vulnerability, and mutual respect. Men must learn to prioritize their partner's needs and desires, embrace vulnerability and emotional intimacy, and reject harmful stereotypes about sex and masculinity. By doing so, couples can cultivate a healthy and fulfilling sex life that strengthens their emotional connection and deepens their bond.

CHAPTER 13

Breaking Free from Toxic Masculinity: A Journey of Growth and Transformation

Breaking free from toxic masculinity is not an easy feat, but it is a journey worth taking for the betterment of yourself and your relationship. It requires a deep commitment to unlearning harmful behaviors and thought patterns, and a willingness to be vulnerable and open to growth and transformation.

This chapter will explore the steps and strategies for breaking free from toxic masculinity, and embarking on a journey of growth and transformation.

1. Acknowledge the problem.

The first step in breaking free from toxic masculinity is acknowledging the problem. You must be honest with yourself about your harmful behaviors, and the impact they have on your relationship. This can be a painful and difficult process, but it is necessary for growth and change.

2. Seek support.

Breaking free from toxic masculinity is not a journey you should undertake alone. Seek out support from trusted friends, family members, or professionals. Joining a men's support group or seeking therapy can be incredibly helpful in providing a safe space to work through your struggles and challenges.

3. Practice self-reflection.

Self-reflection is a powerful tool for growth and transformation. Take time to reflect on your thoughts, feelings, and behaviors, and the impact they have on your relationship. Journaling, meditation, or mindfulness practices can be helpful in developing self-awareness and introspection.

4. Challenge harmful beliefs and behaviors.

Toxic masculinity is often rooted in harmful beliefs and behaviors that have been reinforced by society and culture. Challenge these beliefs and behaviors by questioning their validity, and seeking alternative perspectives. Practice empathy and active listening, and seek to understand the experiences and perspectives of those around you.

5. Embrace vulnerability.

Vulnerability is a key component of breaking free from toxic masculinity. Embrace vulnerability by being open and honest about your feelings, and willing to express them in a healthy and constructive manner. This can help build trust and connection in your relationship, and pave the way for greater intimacy and emotional connection.

6. Practice self-care.

Self-care is critical in breaking free from toxic masculinity. This means taking care of your physical, emotional, and mental well-being. Engage in activities that bring you joy and fulfillment, and prioritize rest, relaxation, and self-reflection.

7. Celebrate your progress.

Breaking free from toxic masculinity is a journey, not a destination. Celebrate your progress along the way, no matter how small. Recognize and acknowledge the positive changes you have made, and use them as motivation to continue growing and evolving.

In conclusion, breaking free from toxic masculinity is a journey that requires commitment, dedication, and hard work. But the rewards are immense – a deeper connection with yourself, your partner, and the world around you. By acknowledging the problem, seeking support, practicing self-reflection, challenging harmful beliefs and behaviors, embracing vulnerability, practicing self-care, and celebrating your progress, you can embark on a journey of growth and transformation, and build a healthier, more fulfilling relationship.

PART 4

Navigating Challenges and Moving Forward

CHAPTER 14

Challenges and Roadblocks: Overcoming Resistance to Change

Even with the best intentions and efforts, overcoming toxic masculinity in a relationship can be a challenging and complex process. Both partners may encounter roadblocks and resistance to change, which can create obstacles to progress and healing. In this chapter, we will explore common challenges that arise when working to dismantle toxic masculinity in relationships and offer strategies for overcoming resistance and moving forward.

1. ***Fear and resistance to change:*** It is common for people to fear change, and

this can be especially true for those who have grown up with traditional gender roles and expectations. Your partner may be resistant to changing their behavior or may be hesitant to engage in the process of dismantling toxic masculinity. It is important to approach this with empathy and understanding, recognizing that change can be scary for anyone. Engage in open and honest communication about your feelings and concerns, and work together to establish a shared vision for your relationship.

2. **Lack of support:** It can be challenging to navigate the process of overcoming toxic masculinity without a supportive community. You may encounter resistance or even ridicule from friends or family members who do not understand or support your efforts. Seek out support from like-minded individuals, whether through therapy, support groups, or

online communities. Surround yourself with people who understand and validate your experiences.

3. ***Triggers and setbacks:*** Overcoming toxic masculinity can be an emotional journey, and it is common to encounter triggers and setbacks along the way. Old patterns and behaviors may resurface, and your partner may struggle to maintain the progress they have made. It is important to recognize that setbacks are a natural part of the process and to approach them with compassion and understanding. Work together to identify triggers and establish strategies for managing them when they arise.

4. ***Lack of resources:*** Overcoming toxic masculinity may require outside resources, such as therapy, books, or workshops. However, these resources can be expensive or difficult to access. If you

112

are struggling to find resources, consider reaching out to non-profit organizations, community centers, or local universities for support. Many organizations offer sliding scale or free services to those in need.

5. **_Perceived loss of power:_** For many men, toxic masculinity is tied to a sense of power and control in their relationships. As they begin to relinquish these harmful behaviors, they may feel as though they are losing power or control. It is important to recognize that healthy relationships are built on mutual respect and equality, not power imbalances. Work together to establish a shared vision of what a healthy relationship looks like, and approach this journey as a collaborative effort rather than a power struggle.

Overcoming toxic masculinity in a relationship can be a challenging and rewarding journey. By recognizing the challenges and roadblocks that may arise and developing strategies for overcoming them, you and your partner can build a stronger, healthier, and more authentic relationship.

CHAPTER 16

Moving Forward Together: Creating a Shared Vision for Your Relationship

Once you and your partner have begun the journey of dismantling toxic masculinity and fostering a healthy relationship, it's important to create a shared vision for your future. This shared vision will help guide your actions, decisions, and interactions with one another as you move forward.

Creating a shared vision begins with a deep understanding of each other's needs, desires, and goals. It's important to openly communicate and listen to one another to gain this understanding. You may find it helpful to set aside dedicated time to have conversations about your shared vision and what each of you hopes to achieve in your relationship.

As you begin to create your shared vision, it's important to keep in mind the principles and values that you've identified as being essential to a healthy and fulfilling relationship. This includes respect, trust, communication, emotional intelligence, and empathy.

It's also important to consider your individual and shared goals. What do you each hope to achieve personally, professionally, and as a couple? What values and principles are most important to you as individuals and as a couple? How can you support each other in achieving these goals and upholding these values?

Once you've identified your individual and shared goals and values, you can begin to create a roadmap for achieving them. This may involve setting concrete goals, developing strategies for achieving them, and identifying the resources and support you'll need along the way.

It's important to remember that creating a shared vision is an ongoing process. As you and your partner continue to grow and change, your vision may also evolve. It's important to revisit your shared vision regularly and make adjustments as needed.

Creating a shared vision can be a powerful tool for overcoming the challenges that may arise as you work to dismantle toxic masculinity in your relationship. It can provide a sense of purpose, direction, and shared responsibility, as well as a sense of hope and optimism for the future.

The Journey Continues: Living and Thriving Beyond Toxic Masculinity

The journey of dismantling toxic masculinity in a relationship is a long and challenging one, but it is a journey worth taking. It requires a deep commitment to personal growth, a willingness to learn from one's mistakes, and a determination to build a healthy and sustainable relationship based on mutual respect, trust, and empathy.

As you embark on this journey, remember that it is not a destination but a continuous process of growth and transformation. There will be ups and downs, successes and setbacks, but what matters is your commitment to keep moving forward and to keep learning and growing together with your partner.

Living and thriving beyond toxic masculinity requires a shift in mindset and a willingness to challenge the harmful beliefs and stereotypes that have been ingrained in us from a young age. It also requires a willingness to be vulnerable and to open up to our partners, to listen to their needs and feelings, and to support each other through the ups and downs of life.

Remember that you are not alone in this journey. There are many resources and communities available to support you, whether it's seeking the guidance of a therapist, joining a support group, or connecting with like-minded individuals online.

The journey towards dismantling toxic masculinity is not easy, but it is a journey that is worth taking. By challenging harmful stereotypes and cultivating healthy behaviors and attitudes, you can build a relationship that is based on love, respect, and equality. So, take the first step towards a healthier and more fulfilling relationship today and embark on this transformative journey together.

Voices of Change: Inspiring Stories of Couples Who Overcame Toxic Masculinity

The journey to overcome toxic masculinity in relationships is not an easy one, but it is a journey worth taking. It is a journey that requires vulnerability, introspection, and a willingness to change. It is a journey that requires the support and understanding of partners, allies, and advocates. But most importantly, it is a journey that requires hope.

In this epilogue, we hear from couples who have taken this journey and emerged stronger and more connected. These inspiring stories of

121

change and transformation serve as a reminder that toxic masculinity is not a permanent state, and that change is possible.

Story 1:

John and Lisa had been together for five years, and their relationship had been marked by John's tendencies towards toxic masculinity. He would often criticize Lisa's choices, belittle her in front of others, and make all major decisions without consulting her. Lisa had tried to talk to John about his behavior, but he would become defensive and shut down any conversation.

Finally, after a particularly bad argument, Lisa decided that she could not continue in the relationship without significant changes. John, realizing that he was about to lose Lisa, agreed to attend counseling to work on his toxic behavior. The couple attended regular counseling sessions for several months, where they learned new communication skills and how to work through conflict in a healthy way.

Through counseling, John was able to see how his behavior had been damaging to the relationship and to Lisa. He learned how to listen actively and communicate his needs and desires without resorting to aggression or belittling Lisa. Lisa, in turn, learned how to set healthy boundaries and express her needs in a constructive manner.

Today, John and Lisa have a thriving relationship built on mutual respect and trust. They credit counseling with helping them to recognize and overcome toxic masculinity, and they continue to practice the skills they learned in counseling to maintain a healthy and fulfilling relationship.

Story 2:

Samantha and Tom had been together for ten years when they realized that Tom's toxic masculinity was a major issue in their relationship. Tom would often become angry and aggressive when things didn't go his way, and he would frequently shut down emotionally, leaving Samantha feeling alone and unheard.

At Samantha's urging, the couple began attending couples therapy to address Tom's toxic behavior. In therapy, they explored the root causes of Tom's behavior, including his upbringing and societal expectations of masculinity. With the help of their therapist, Tom was able to develop a greater sense of emotional intelligence and empathy towards Samantha's experiences.

Through therapy, Tom was able to learn how to express his emotions in a healthy way, and to listen actively to Samantha's concerns. Samantha, in turn, learned how to be more assertive in expressing her own needs, and to set boundaries when necessary.

Today, Samantha and Tom have a much healthier relationship, built on mutual trust and respect. They continue to practice the skills they learned in therapy to ensure that toxic masculinity never again threatens their relationship.

Story 3:

Jasmine and Ryan had been together for only a few months when they realized that Ryan's toxic masculinity was a major issue in their relationship. Ryan would frequently make derogatory comments about women, and he would often pressure Jasmine into sexual acts she was uncomfortable with.

Jasmine was hesitant to speak up at first, fearing that she would lose Ryan if she challenged his behavior. However, with the encouragement of a close friend, she decided to confront Ryan about his behavior.

At first, Ryan became defensive and dismissive of Jasmine's concerns. However, over time, he began to understand the impact of his behavior on their relationship. With the help of a counselor, Ryan was able to develop a greater sense of empathy and self-awareness, and he committed to working on his toxic behavior.

Through counseling, Ryan was able to learn how to communicate his desires in a healthy way, and to respect Jasmine's boundaries. Jasmine, in turn, learned how to be more assertive in expressing her own needs, and to hold Ryan accountable for his behavior.

Today, Jasmine and Ryan have a much healthier relationship, built on mutual trust and respect. They credit their counselor with helping them to recognize and overcome toxic masculinity, and they continue to practice the skills they learned in counseling to ensure a healthy and fulfilling relationship.

Printed in Dunstable, United Kingdom